REA

FRIENDS
OF ACPL

ALLEN COUNTY PUBLIC LIBRARY
3 1833 03836 2577

OCT 3 2002

Arrival Time

D1114456

Arrival
Time

a journal of love

Carol Osterlund
and
Robert Sellers

FITHIAN PRESS, SANTA BARBARA, CALIFORNIA, 2000

"Glacier Talk" first appeared in Volume 33, No. 1, the spring issue of *Sandcutters,* published by the Arizona State Poetry Society.

"Sunday in Sydney" received Honorable Mention from the Australian Poetry Society in 1995.

"The Wolf Who Cried 'Boy'" and "Cashmere Sweaters and Other Friends" won awards at the Santa Barbara Writers Conference.

Copyright © 2000 by Carol Osterlund and Robert Sellers
All rights reserved
Printed in the United States of America

Published by Fithian Press
A division of Daniel and Daniel, Publishers, Inc.
Post Office Box 1525
Santa Barbara, CA 93102
www.danielpublishing.com

LIBRARY OF CONGRESS CATALOGING-IN-PUBLICATION DATA
Osterlund, Carol (date)
    Arrival time: a journey of love / by Carol Osterlund and Robert Sellers.
       p. cm.
    ISBN 1-56474-329-2 (alk. paper)
    1. Love poetry, American. 2. Voyages and travels—Poetry. 3. Aging—poetry. 4. Aged—
Poetry. I. Sellers, Robert, (date) II. Title.
    PS3565.S818 A89 2000
811'.54—dc21   99-050459
                                                                     CIP

We dedicate this book to
our children and grandchildren
with our love and gratitude for the way you light our journey

We wish you joy of dancing wave,
The freedom of a gull,
Wisdom stored like treasure
Deep in ancient hull.

May you have dreams to follow dreams
Like sand upon the sand
And faith to hear the widening seas
From shells within your hand.

Contents

Part III: We Pause to Reflect (Epilogue)

Acknowledgments

We are grateful to the staff and fellow students of the Santa Barbara Writers Conference. For ten years we have been eager participants in this yearly celebration of writers and writing.

Perie Longo leads the morning workshop on poetry. Her grace and inspiration carry us into new areas of creativity.

Bill Wilkins conducts the afternoon session. We appreciate his love for concise writing and his ability to help us achieve this essence of thought.

Dorothy Lykes, a fellow student at the conference, teaches an ongoing class in Scottsdale, Arizona. Under her tutelage we explore poems of varied forms and respond to her challenge that we express our changing emotions in ever-evolving poetic forms.

Arrival Time

Robert's Prologue

I always believed I would be the first to die. My wife, Libby, had all the longevity genes going for her. My mother died when I was seven and no male on my side of the family lived beyond his fifties. Now, I was the one who had to confront loneliness, left behind in a house full of treasures and memories from forty-seven years of a wonderful marriage.

During our life together, Libby always wrote of her feelings. The last year, as a way to deal with the rigors of chemotherapy, she worked with her writings and journal entries, copying these and her poems to floppy discs. The second morning after the funeral I awoke at four in the morning, sat down at the computer and opened her files. I was in awe of the depth with which she recorded reflections of our life together, her illness, and the acceptance of approaching death. I hoped that I would find a message to help deal with my loss. It was probably there but not expressed concisely in the few words my engineering approach to life would like.

Maybe this search and perhaps wanting to find healing convinced me that I should write the story of our love affair. I wrote of our first dates and thought I was doing well until I found her diary. We remembered the same events, but my memories were surprisingly different. I struggled with recording both of our feelings. I shared my frustrations with a young woman who had called one evening to express her concern over Libby's death. She answered that I should not write about our romance but tell my own story. I started over and began describing my childhood in Los Angeles during the 1920's. I enrolled in a creative writing class at Fresno City College and an English grammar class at a nearby high school. Both proved helpful. With the encouragement of the students and teachers I continued writing, and the pain of loss diminished.

I knew I must reenter the mainstream of life. I continued with the spiritual growth group in our church. I attended two grief support groups but did not find the help I sought. I looked at the treasures in the house and garden, the accumulation of years. I concluded the real treasures were the people who had used our home as a sanctuary. I realized I did not want to become a docent at a shrine. Living with my daughter or either son did not appeal to me. I doubted I would find anyone to share my life like the wonderful wife I had lost.

Callers came to express their concern. I accepted several invitations to dinner. In August, I attended a week-long retreat in northern California for which Libby and I had enrolled six months before. I went prepared to join old friends in singing her praises, expecting to share an ongoing memorial to the woman who had blessed our lives. Instead, the participants turned their love and attention to me. They made me aware of my own individual gifts and all that I could bring to a new relationship. I came home determined to find a companion. The question I faced was where could I find someone to share my resurgent passion for life.

Miraculously, friends, Chuck and Joy McCaleb, invited me to lunch in Los Banos, and this was the beginning and the end of the search. In the next months, Carol captured my heart with her enthusiasm for life as expressed in her letters and phone calls. By October 31st, I was certain. I told my therapist, my doctor, the bank teller, and anyone who would listen that I was going to San Jose to meet the woman I would marry.

Carol's Prologue

In 1968 I spent one part of a day, seven hours, with Libby Sellers, and it changed my life. I was attending an all-day retreat for women, sponsored by the state conference of our church. I met Libby's glance as the group leader requested that we each find a partner. We both smiled, nodded, realized we had chosen each other. We exchanged brief outlines of our lives. Our homes were 150 miles apart, hers in Fresno, mine in San Jose. I was thirty-nine, Libby, ten years older.

We laughed as we discovered that we were both daughters of carpenters, married to engineers. Libby had two sisters as I did. We each had one daughter then two sons, with ten years separating the oldest and youngest.

We became intensely involved in the program of the retreat. It was easy to share sacred beliefs and private dreams. We discovered a mutual love for writing poetry. By the end of the day, I knew I had met a woman who could become a close friend. As a way of continuing the experience, we were asked to make a commitment to one another. Libby promised to pray that I would continue to be creative, that my poems would enrich others and please me.

For a moment I could not answer. I saw a seasoned, wise woman with an easy grace, brown eyes, and soft dark hair beginning to gray. Just any vow would never do. As she waited, my words came.

"Whenever I think of you, Libby, I will love you."

A few days following the retreat, I received a letter from Libby. She enclosed a poem she had written to me. I responded. We wrote a few times. Then, my father was hospitalized with heart disease. Mother grew more dependent. My marriage of twenty-two years was failing. In the midst of all the demands, I lost close touch with Libby, but remembered my vow.

Because we were both active at the state level of church leadership, we had many mutual friends. Libby worked in Christian education. I gave my attention to the outreach program, trying to translate theological goals into a lay person's language. Often in a casual conversation or in a meeting of a conference committee, I would hear her name. My reaction was always the same, "When you see Libby, tell her I love her."

In the next year my father died. My marriage ended. I assumed full responsibility for the care of my mother. In 1974 I remarried, a loving, wonderful man, Erik Osterlund. For fourteen years, life overflowed with his career, my writing, and the intricacies of our blended family. In May of 1988, mother died at 92, a peaceful, gentle passing. A month later, doctors told my husband he had lung cancer, already far advanced. Six weeks after the diagnosis, Erik smiled at me for the last time.

A few weeks later, in early September, my friend, Joy, mentioned that she and her husband, Chuck, were meeting Robert Sellers for lunch. His wife, Libby, after an illness of a year, had died of lymphoma in May. My response was automatic.

"When you see Robert, tell him, I always loved Libby."

Asked to explain the message, I told Joy the story, which she repeated to Robert. His reaction to my dual loss was intense, wondered if it would be all right if he wrote to me. Joy assured him that I would welcome any correspondence. In September, I answered Robert's first letter but by then, he was visiting his daughter in Connecticut. Somehow, in the overflow of accumulated mail, my note went astray. Seven weeks later he learned from Joy that I had responded, and immediately called my number.

That Sunday evening I attended a grief support group. As I entered the house, the telephone rang. I picked it up and heard Robert's voice for the first time.

"Hello, this is Bob Sellers. I am sorry, but I didn't get your letter."

I don't remember feeling surprised by his call. His voice belonged in my life. For the next ten days we wrote letters, most of them crossing in the mail, and our long-distance calls increased. I trusted Robert. When I awoke, lonely at three in the morning, I knew I could phone him. We talked, easily responding to the other's feelings.

November first was the earliest day we were both free; I invited Robert for lunch. He drove the 150 miles, arrived at my house carrying flowers, popcorn, soap bubble liquid and poetry. I looked into his blue eyes. When he put his arms around me, my crazy, lopsided world clicked into place.

By January, we were living together in San Jose. Those first months were a strange combination of falling in love and sharing our grief. We always allowed the other full access to the past. We honored each other's stories, our personal journeys, the joys and sorrows we each had known. We cherished old memories as we created new ones.

One afternoon, when we had been together about six months, I sorted through a box of keepsakes. Among the cards and photographs, I found the letter from Libby following that 1968 retreat. I showed Robert her note and the poem she had written. He recognized the poetry, but never knew for whom it was intended. I had come full circle. That day marked an end to the pain. Libby's poem was both a benediction to the past and a blessing for the future.

Together, Robert and I read her words. I looked up from the page and said,

"I always loved Libby."

The Power and the Glory Forever

Once in a while but not very often
                we may meet a person with whom we
                        feel   free
                        in empathy   in sympathy
with whom we can be Ourselves
                        honest   unjudged   secure

And no matter what we say
        it won't be met with a   raised eyebrow   or a frown
                a change of subject   or a turn away
        a self-conscious laugh   a judgmental statement
        it will be listened to
                coming from us
                        commented on   cherished as
Coming from Me!
        which frees me to want to hear
                what you have to say
                      to care for and empathize with you.
Perhaps if what's between us is really real
        you can then be yourself, too
                honest   unjudged   secure
And this then is where God comes in LOVE
The beauty, the joy of this shared feeling is inestimable
        if it only happens once with two
                It becomes a bit of the POWER that
                can never be taken away from them.
        They are a little closer to BECOMING REAL PERSONS
        and a little closer to BEING CHRISTIAN
The frightening thing is that if we don't "leave our windows open"
        we may never come by this POWER
        and the GLORY FOREVER AND EVER. AMEN

Libby Sellers, 1968

The Early Letters

September 4, 1988, to November 14, 1988

"…until Tuesday when I see you smile."

Carol

"…the door swings wide without my knock."

Robert

September 4, 1988

Dear Carol:

I have just returned to Fresno after having lunch with Chuck and Joy. I am suddenly aware how small and yet infinitely large the world is all at the same time. When they shared your recent loss and your memory of Libby at a workshop in Fresno at least twenty years ago, I was in such a state of wonder that tears came to my eyes.

It may seem strange to you for me to be writing as I honestly don't remember if we ever met. I am aware that we both share a recent loss to the villain cancer. I want to extend my heartfelt sympathy to you and to share my wish that time and people will bring to you as they have to me, a healing of understanding love. Many things have happened to me since Libby's passing in May. I am truly amazed at the recollections, stories and just plain vanilla love that have been sent and given to me.

You may not know but Libby was a writer and left me with a legacy of diaries, journals, poems, scrapbooks etc. Chuck and Joy may share that I started writing a book to somehow assemble all her collected writings. I was having a rough time, until someone suggested that I make it my story. Now it is beginning to come together. I have worked through my own childhood and the years of our courtship. Fortunately I have Libby's early years well chronicled by her mother and her diaries through college.

All the way driving home from Los Banos I was sure that I could find something in writing about your visit to Fresno. So far no luck. This was the start of her transition from an impersonal to a personal theology. Writing of this transition is going to be difficult. I would like sometime to have the opportunity of talking to you about this time in her life over dinner or lunch.

Thank you for letting me share with you,
my sympathy and affection.
Bob

The Lost Letter

September 9, 1988

Dear Bob,

Many years ago I wrote a line of poetry—

"I will love you yesterday as much as I have loved you tomorrow."

So often I am aware of time circling back. The period when I met Libby was for me, also, marked with intense personal change. How strange and thought provoking that an encounter years ago may bring new friendship in days still to come.

I do not believe that we ever met. Chuck and Joy praised your writing. I would be thrilled if you would share some with me. Incidentally, your phrase "just plain vanilla love" was pure delight.

I believe I have made progress on this journey called "grief." My own writing supports and keeps me aware of feelings. I would appreciate knowing how you have coped to arrive at a "healing of understanding love."

Joy mentioned that you planned a trip soon—so call or write when you are free. If we meet halfway, lunch would be best. For fun I enclose a picture of Erik and me taken five years ago. My hair is gray now, not frosted, but the smile is much the same. I also include one of my poems. It, too, seems strangely appropriate.

Most sincerely,
Carol

Footsteps on a Far Shore

I have climbed a thousand hills
And never marked the way,
Nor stopped to talk with leaf or bird
Nor mourned the passing day.

I have walked an endless beach,
Left footprints in a row.
When time and tide bore them off,
I did not watch them go.

Now days converge. I learn of hills
And join each leaf in prayer,
Then follow birds to some far shore
To find my footprints there.

Carol

October 23, 1988

Dear Carol:

I do not understand all that happens in the world. The disappearance of your letter has added to that lack of understanding. I left for Connecticut to be with my daughter and her husband, shortly after visiting with Chuck and Joy in Los Banos. My neighbor brings in my mail and is very good about it. I got home and found Chuck and Joy's letters, and I am sure I would have discovered and cherished any first class mail among the junk.

As I told you on the phone I have berated myself for being presumptuous in writing. To find out from Joy that my letter was well received brought all kinds of good feelings. Then talking with you was very special. Now I can look forward to meeting you the weekend of November 4th.

Enclosed is a copy of the book of poetry that Libby put together and I recently had reprinted. I have also enclosed a copy of "I Don't Need to Understand About the Roses" which has been very interesting to share as I get so many different interpretations of the message. I haven't shared it with another poet so it will be interesting to discuss it with you. I am writing a book of our life together and have been using a stanza of her poetry with each chapter. So far I feel comfortable with my selections. When I get into the years of our transition to a personal theology I may have a harder time. I am still dealing with the war years and am anxious to move on, but I keep finding material that should be included. I am beginning to learn that rewriting is far more time consuming than putting down the original thoughts. Sharing with you some of my questions about the whole process will be very helpful.

I am attending a writing class at Fresno City College. The teacher and students are encouraging me to expand my remembrances into the story. I am learning what a personal essay is all about. Somehow from high school and college I got the impression that essays went with fame. It is fascinating to read the stories written by members of the class as we are all kind of average people.

I am so sorry that your letter was lost.

With affection,
Bob

I Do Not Need to Understand About the Roses

In the ebb and flow of life—nothing remains static
    As it once was or might become.
Life continues in its ever fluctuating role
    Bringing to fruition—blooming lustily
        Going out   coming in
            Creeping away   turning its back   letting go.

Life pursues, regresses—touches me, and roughly flings away
    Buffets—blooms   withers—dies in senseless disarray.
Understanding lost, covered over, buried.
    Cursed, I cry out…
GOD   you don't make any sense at all.

Anger overwhelms me   confronts me   mocks me
    Willing me to inaction.
        The way is dark—and ultimately
            I am left alone.

There are no more "what-might-have-beens"…
    Things unsaid—warmed-over cliches mouthed.
        I spit them out
            Rub them under my feet. They do not disappear.
Love, pick them up   dust them off
    Turn dead ashes into roses for me
        And let my tears come.
            God, let them come—sweet saltiness
        In my mouth   down my cheeks

And love does come—overwhelmingly, it seems.
    There never was   never will be   only IS.
        Understanding incomplete
            Nothing ever finished   only just begun
These regrets return to kick me in the face.…
    Make blood of my tears
        Regretting so consumes me
            Yet is lifted from me—by LOVE?

Life ebbs and flows and Death can only be
    a continuation dissolving regret?
There may be no carrying over into the "next life"
    Anything of this—except love.
        Only Love evens the score—cancels my debt
           Allows me new life; says YES and lets me go.
Only LOVE?—only love
    And I do not need to understand about the roses.

Libby Sellers, February 27, 1973

Tuesday 6:00 A.M.
October 25, 1988

Dear Bob:
What a nice voice you have! I wanted to talk longer, but I don't know you well enough to find the questions to ask.

What are your dreams? What makes you laugh? How do you cope with the sudden rush of tears? Do you like to plan ahead, making anticipation part of the experience? Do you enjoy being spontaneous? Would you like to talk all night, walk the beach at sunrise and wish on a starfish? Have you ever dreamed of flying to Lake Louise for a few days? Do you like the way Doris Day sang "It's Magic" and Harry James played "I Had the Craziest Dream"?

I do regret that the "postal pixies" purloined my response to your beautiful letter. I did delight in your "plain vanilla love." And I look forward to sharing some feelings from that charismatic time when I met Libby.

For a while there, when you did not answer, I thought, "Well, I did it again!" I worry that I tend to be too intense, to come on too strongly for most people. It's just that I cherish new experience. If Erik's death taught anything it is to treasure the present moment and be a good steward of each day of life. I enclose another poem of mine which says if we do not respond, we are the losers.

So Bob, be the person you are. What a joy it will be to know you better. New friendship hangs on such a fragile gossamer thread. But what a gift to live this precious shining moment. Whether that is the extent or we weave a fabric of shared experience, it is worth the doing.

I am excited and count the days to see you smile.

All my best,
Carol

All Hallow's Eve

All Hallow's Eve.
A knock outside.
I open the door of my heart.
You stand before me,
Masked in friendship.

"Trick or Treat," you say.
Now I must decide what my response will be.
Shall I offer sweet and gentle softness of love?
If I do, what will it mean to you?
Will you add it to the other goodies in your bag,
Still to wander lost and lonely through the night,
Looking for that one perfect gift
Only your own faith can find?

Yet, if I refuse,
The trick will be on me.
I will be locked in a room
Of my own apartness
Behind doors
That may not swing so wide
Again.

Carol

October 27, 1988

Dear Carol,

I was going to start by writing that you would never know how much your letter meant to me. Of course you will know and if I didn't tell you adequately on the phone I certainly will on Tuesday. You ask what are my dreams? A large part of my dreams lately have been that there would be someone in my life like you that would write and talk in such a caring way. These are the conscious and semi-conscious dreams. The deep sleep dreams at this time elude me on awakening. Perhaps because I find myself wide awake with more anxiety than I would like. Time will undoubtedly correct this loss.

What makes me laugh?—I can see the humor in most anything if there is any there. Mostly I laugh at silly kids and cats. I have a good outlook on life and love to have fun and be with optimistic people. I am well aware that life can't be happy-go-lucky all the time.

I am the original planner. I research a trip sometimes so well that we used to disappoint ourselves when we didn't get to see everything as planned. Later, we found we knew as much about what we missed as those who had been there. Planning to me is almost, but not quite, as much fun as doing. Yes I would love to talk all night. I might go to sleep but then I wake up and am really raring to go again in the early morning. My kids called me C.O.D. (crack of dawn). I would love to walk on the beach at sunrise, mid-day, or sunset and even at night. I'll wish on any kind of star.

As I told you, Delta has a wonderful package for Lake Louise and let's do it when it gets warmer. How about Amsterdam and Vienna around the first of March?

I love "It's Magic"and "I Had the Craziest Dream." My life before Libby was torch songs, the more tragic the better, then even until six weeks ago all that I wanted to hear were love songs. Then it was back to the torch songs. So now I need someone like you to bring the magic back. How about that "Old Black Magic"?

Considering the lost letter, we should both learn the lesson that self-reproach serves no useful purpose. Put it down to a bad break that cost us five wonderful weeks. You can't be too intense for me and I hope I am not for you. Now that we know each other by letter, telephone and soon in person, nothing need be left to the fickle finger of fate. Maybe fate has already taken over to bring us together as in the Latin: *Ducunt volentem fata, nolentem trahunt:* "The fates lead him who will; him who won't they drag." I don't know the first thing about Latin or I would have changed the him to us.

Thank you for the poem. I am haunted by "All Hallow's Eve" and enclosed is my response to it.

I will close with a big dish of plain vanilla love—this time with chocolate sauce, a dab of whipped cream, a bright red cherry and a few nuts sprinkled on top.

Much love,
Bob

Trick or Treat

She thinks that with faith I'll find
The perfect gift I desperately seek.
Yet I still walk the lonely street.

All Hallow's Eve, I stand at her door.
Empty bag in one hand, other poised to knock.
Then I withdraw with cautious fear.

How can she know the truth behind
My mask of friendship, pleasant smile?
A vacant sign will never show
The emptiness of heart.

Surely she will see into my empty bag,
That I have asked many times for love,
Been turned away without a treat.

The door swings wide without my knock.
She is there willing to give love,
Not in fear of trick and not in fun.

Love so proffered
Does not go in my empty bag.
It goes straight in my vacant heart.
I walk the lonely street no more.

Bob

Thursday, October 27, 1988

Dear Bob...
Not really a letter...only random thoughts demanding expression.

What do you suppose happened to my first letter? Perhaps it was tucked inside a circular urging you to vote yes on proposition 104, scanned quickly and tossed away. Did it fall with a plop into the mailbox of a stranger, who opened it, read the words and wondered what manner of crazy-lady poet wrote,

"Yes.... I would love to talk to you about Libby."

"Yes.... I would treasure the experience of reading what you have written."

"Yes.... Let's talk about twenty years ago and yesterday and tomorrow, life and death and how to put ideas on paper."

But nothing is ever really lost. I still own the feelings and, really all my letter said...yes.

I love the poetry Libby wrote, the passion for life compressed into disciplined lines. How sad I never read her poems until now. I wish we had shared quiet times, sat across a sunlit kitchen table, talked about mid-life crisis, growing children and new-old dreams. We might have laughed and cried together. We might have been good friends.

I would have echoed her words, "Who can understand roses?" Or how life follows death or why joy is intrinsic in sorrow, and often loving means letting go lest we destroy what we hold too close.

What a range of emotions in one little book of poems...the tragedy of dear love becoming illusive, the hard work in rebuilding the shaky structures of relationship, the need to be known, to be cherished.

I loved her response to early blossoms, Sunday by the lake, the warm cuddly care for the cat sleeping on the bed. The poem you marked.... the ephemeral telephone conversation contrasted with the reality and pleasure of a letter. Thank you for the gift of this glimpse of Libby.

Oh! I love words! And words can be such witches, transforming black letters on a white page into mirrors of self, calling out emotion, creating new hopes from buried memories.

Please Bob, don't be concerned if I seem to write too intensely. I know for each of us many doors wait to be opened. I hope I approach each unknown one with courage, knowing I will make many wrong choices. But I rejoice in my human self and only hope to continue to take responsibility for each action, never see myself as a victim and learn from the mistakes.

So if I take your hand in friendship it is with no expectation other than we will share what is right for us to share.

(This I had written before your phone call.... How fantastic that you will drive over on Tuesday. It is almost as exciting as flying to Lake Louise.)

Until Tuesday...
All my best,
Carol

Friday, October 28th

Dear Robert,

I hasten to mail this note, I worry that I was so bemused by spontaneity of your phone calls that my directions may have been off. Even at my best I sometimes say left when I mean right. So here's a map Erik drew for a past party…it should bring you to my door.

Perhaps it is more fitting that we meet on "All Saints' Day" instead of the day before. I struggle with the reason for the illusion…maybe because our relationships with our spouses brought us to this point where it is appropriate to meet and be friends.

I enclose yet another poem from twenty years ago. Since this time, the autumn leaf has been a talisman for me…seeing the beauty and challenge in change, accepting endings as part of each new beginning.

Because this is a new start, may I call you Robert? I like the soft sound of it, rather than the abruptness of Bob. Somehow, your proper name fits the way I think of you.

No time to write more. I'm off to the post office and the grocery store. My refrigerator contains three unopened bottles of wine, half a carton of yogurt, a papaya and four carrots. My son, Brian, will be here for dinner so…. I must replenish!

Have a happy weekend…until Tuesday when I see you smile….

All my best,
Carol

Autumn Leaf

I would be a maple leaf,
High on tallest tree,
No more to wear naive green
For dreams have followed bird flight.
Winds call my name.
I lean toward light
And yet caress the rain,
Merge into the beauty
Of this wildly colored day.
I am touched with crimson.
All the gold of autumn
Centers in my heart.

You,
Whom I have loved,
How long will you be content
To stay, unchanged,
Green upon the evergreen?

What can you know of glory?
What can you know of pain?

Carol

5:00 A.M.
October 30, 1988

Dear Carol,

You can see from the time on the heading that I am as bad as the poor cows that can't adjust to the time change. I had a good night's sleep after the wild night of anticipation the night before. But I awoke at what I thought was 5:30 only to find it to be 4:30. Lay in bed for a few minutes and suddenly realized that like the cows I was so full I needed to be milked. So here goes.

I went to the housewarming party for the lady across the street. There were football games on the TV which all the men watched in the living room and the women gathered around a big table just off the kitchen. As each single woman came to the party, she joined the group in the kitchen. When a couple came, it was man to the TV, woman to the kitchen. I suddenly was very aware that the living room was not where I wanted to be now or in the future. Everything that I read seems to indicate that this is the structure for most people. No way do I want any part of such a life style. Without really knowing a single soul I would wager that you and I are closer on a spiritual and intellectual level than any of the others—man and wife, mother and daughter, aunt and niece, cousin and cousin, best friends. If I made such an observation and told them that we haven't even met face-to-face it would blow their minds. Never could they understand the eagerness with which I look forward to our meeting and the unlimited potential of the sharing of the riches that we hold for each other.

I could never be a loner unless I just wanted to watch TV, have banal conversations, and listen to chatter. I know with all of me that you are the person that would understand, listen, and respond, coaxing out of me my real feelings and desires. I do not know why this is of paramount importance at this time in my life, but it is. I am not a strong person. I have no desire to dominate, to glorify my ego. I have always felt that my greatest need is to be needed, and under all the bravado, I am very needy. I won't find what I seek by being in the place I was last night. I belong—talking to, writing to, enjoying the companionship of a wonderful person like you.

My feeling like a cow, I have decided, comes from the fact that I have feasted in my life in the greenest of pastures. If I liken milk to love, giving love on a regular basis permits me to take on more nourishment from the world around me and give more love every day. I was suddenly taken from the milking shed and turned out to freshen. I am now ready to again give nurture and as a cow I am so structured that it must be coaxed from me. If it is not taken from me, it will produce great discomfort and gradually my ability to give will decrease until I am dry. You wouldn't let that happen to me would you? Daylight or Standard or any time, I'm ready.

4:00 P.M.

I wrote the above, finally giving in to the cats meowing (they don't understand time changes any better than cows) and took time out for their breakfast and mine. Then the glory and wonder of your phone call and my day really began. When the bell rang I prayed it was you and my prayer was answered. I keep saying how much you mean to me, and in forty two and a half hours I will tell you in person. Why must time go so slowly when one is so anxious?

There is so much to talk about that it will take a thousand nights. How about a new book "A Thousand American Nights" by Bob and Carol? We will dedicate it to Ted and Alice.

The cats are back like faithful cows. They think it's five P.M., and I can't convince them it's only four.

Much love,
Robert

5:30 A.M.
October 31, 1988

Dear Carol:
The world has just completed the slowest turn that it ever made in space and we are one day and few hours from that moment in the orientation of earth, sun, and stars when we will at last be able to look into each other's eyes. It was a slow turn despite having things to do and a wonderful experience of hearing "Elijah" presented by a very talented group at First Congregational Church.

I awoke again from a dream of which I had no recall to go into a conscious dream or fantasy wherein I attempted to deal with my frustrations of the last few days when I am in relationship with people. I fantasized that I have over the last six months built around me a cocoon from threads of love and caring furnished by many people and those drawn from my own resources. I am ready to emerge but in coming out I am suddenly a little scared. After the performance of "Elijah" we went to have a spaghetti dinner in the patio of the church. I was in the company of Sigrid, a younger woman, and her eleven-year-old daughter and the daughter's friend. Of course I immediately was greeted by old friends. We left that church probably seventeen years ago and the parting was painful. But the greeting when we went back from time to time was always the same: "We have missed you," inferring that we really belonged there—never asking to find out where we were in our life. Last night everyone asked how was I doing. I haven't figured out how to answer that one yet. Obviously I was doing fine as I was in a good place.

The encounter that stands out most was the last of many. A couple, who were once close friends, came up and I introduced Sigrid, telling them that she was transferring her membership to their church. I thought they would be interested as they had been members for years. I told them that Sigrid and I were attending a spiritual growth group that was meeting in their fireside room and that the membership of the group was about half and half from the two churches. He then countered with the information that one should pursue their interests and that he and his wife subscribed to cable TV so that they could get the sports not for the HBO, Cinemax, etc. That blew both Sigrid's and my mind to the point of near collapse. I looked at him and shook hands realizing that their church is not a place for me.

After running all that through my mind in bed this morning, I went from being in a cocoon to living in Shangri-la. (Thank you for bringing that vision to me). I have ventured out of my safe haven many times. At first it was hard to leave home and travel alone but that I worked out with myself. The last few major trips I have not minded the leaving but dreaded coming back. Now I am about to leave for the greatest adventure for me in a long, long time. Are each of the experiences of the last two days telling me something? Like I don't need this life style anymore and I really don't have to come back. I want to come into your life and live in the world that you and I build. As we discussed on the telephone, each of us brings unbelievable riches from our years of growing. This new relationship will make us the greatest team yet. Looking down the road to San Jose, there is no tunnel and no snow as in Shangri-la, but I worry I might suddenly age. Then my heart, soul and mind reassure me that with your love and help that will never happen.

With those thoughts, fantasies, and a lot of promises I come to you with open heart, mind, and soul, each running on empty, but eagerly anticipating being filled to overflowing.

I love you,
Robert

November 3, 1988

To Robert
After all the phone calls and letters...we meet.

You arrived early Tuesday morning, waited until nearly ten o'clock before driving to my house. Did I tell you I was just as anxious. I woke early, prepared chicken curry salads for lunch (how could I guess, one of your favorites). The table was set for two and a small fire blazed in the hearth. I watched you walk across the patio, opened the door before you touched the bell.

I believe in that first moment we both realized we gazed on a face we would love. Does it happen like this for other couples?

You asked on the phone what I remembered of that first hour. You went back to the car, returned carrying liquid for soap bubbles, a bouquet of flowers, popcorn and poetry. I smile when I think of the sparkle in your blue eyes when you said you tried to think of everything that would delight me.

I offered you a cup of coffee and you asked if I would marry you. Then we talked and I explained I was caught in a crazy financial situation which at this time a legal marriage would only complicate. Again, I suggested a cup of coffee and you responded with an invitation to a cruise through the Panama Canal in January. Were you surprised that I answered yes so quickly?

I remember our strolling around the neighborhood. I close my eyes and see that perfect yellow rose in the garden on the next street. Was it after lunch, after I read your last letters, the poetry, that I suggested we drive to Santa Cruz, have dinner on the pier, watch our first sunset over the ocean? You were so sweet to do anything I wished. On the way we stopped in the redwood park. I don't miss you so much now, for I can feel my hand in yours as we walked through the grove of trees in the slanted light of late afternoon.

I felt so giddy. I have never before experienced absolute freedom. You seemed to understand my need to crowd so many things I love into one magic day. Why? I know we have only begun. You promise, as I do if the fates are kind, we will have years together. So I will wait until next time, when I see you smile.

With my love,
Carol

November 14, 1988

My darling Carol,

The days were so empty just a little more than three weeks ago. Now because of you they overflow with possibilities. It was hard to take when you drove on in the rain yesterday, as I took the Hollister turnoff. I guess we are right in keeping our promises to spend Thanksgiving and Christmas with our respective families, but I shall miss you. In the meantime let's spend as much time together as possible. My flight to Minneapolis doesn't leave until Saturday morning. Thursday's writing class has been canceled so I am at loose ends from Tuesday morning until Friday morning. Any ideas? I am sure you want to be at your women's group Friday afternoon. I promise to leave before noon.

Like you, I love to relive the hours we have shared. I am glad you were comfortable meeting in Monterey. It was a special place for you and Erik as it was for Libby and me. Now we have made memories of our own. Point Lobos was a great spot for a picnic. I had forgotten November 11th was a holiday, but we did find the perfect shaded table.

Isn't it amazing that on the day I put a ring on your finger, we each had brought a marriage poem to read to the other. Did I tell you that Libby's was written after thirty-two years of our marriage for a couple who had decided to wed after several failed experiences. I cannot remember when you wrote yours, but I do know, both were special to share. As I reread them I find that each underscores our belief in trust and unconditional love.

Let's promise that words will continue to bless our life. Let's leave notes for each other, read aloud passages from books, write in our notebooks private thoughts to share. No way will I forget the precious moments as we pledged our unending love. Just like you said on the phone we are in a different place with each other and for now I am wrapped in a blanket of love and just want to go with all the good feelings.

Just finished sharing my happiness with Fred and Mary Ann Primrose, the couple who live in Murphys, and they were overjoyed. They were both so aware of the love and joy in my voice. When I told them that we might be coming to your place in nearby Forest Meadows they were wild in anticipation. They even volunteered to bring us supplies with their four wheel drive as snow level was down to 4000 feet up there last night. We are going to bring so much happiness to so many in addition to ourselves. What a fantastic life we will have!!

With all my love,
Robert

A Marriage Poem

"And you shall become as one," the Marriage Vow says
    We shall remain alone,
But our word says, No, we shall not be as one....
    Separated by the love we share,
    Separated by the caring that is ours
    The caring that surrounds us
        supports us
        is forever there.

My word, your word, that is love
    Is
    Is forever there
    Is forever the caring
        that allows us our separation
        that allows us our freedom
        that allows me to be me
            you to be you.

Word that is love does not make us one
    My strength is in me is in you
        is in my separation
        is in my connection
    My connection with you is ever tenuous
    Is up for renewal every hour that I live.
    I become one with you
        only in the strength
            of my freedom to be.

The very tenuousness of this connection
    Makes of it a preciousness
    That very few can ever see
    That very few lovers allow to exist.

They do not know that their goal on loving
    Need not be to Become-One-Forever
    But to become one each time it happens
    Within the freedom of each time.

I need to be free of you
    for me to freely love you
    O Lord, whose word I love,
    I learned this from You
        So surely this is true for me.

You need to be free of me
    and make your life your own
    For then you and our love will grow
    and be renewed each time we are together.

     Libby   *6/20/73*

Promise

I place my hand
In yours,
Feel the wide expanse of palm,
Gentle roughness
Of long fingers
Folded around mine.

If I move
From your touch
Your hand would open.
I could fly,
Return
Fly again.

I choose this homecoming,
The warmth
Of belonging.
As your ring
Circles my finger
We turn
Walk
Hand in hand.

Carol

Along the Way

1989–1999

"Every road leads to daffodils."

—Carol

"Let's get up and go, be part of the wonderful."

—Robert

A Warm Reply

Falling in love comes
When you are scared
Of eating alone.
When there is fire in the devil's well
You feel the ribbon beside the empty bank, and
Snapdragons grow in the pumpkins and squash.

Balloons on strings haven't brought results
So I cut them loose, tie a feather
To the leaf and off they go into the wind.
Then at least the birds will know
The waiting has begun.

The warmth of your reply chases
Away the chill of Halloween night.
I reach into the sky to capture
A bright balloon borne by a flock of
Swallows and find to my delight
A roll of dimes for my empty bank.

Robert

Arrival Time

That November day
You walked toward me
I moved into the circle of your arms
It was like coming home

From different paths
Through joy and loss
We met
To share these late life years

Now
Air flight ends
Seat belt signs turn off
We are free to step into
Zimbabwe, Vienna
Ship whistles sound as
We dock in Acapulco
Barcelona or the harbor of New York

We return to familiar rooms
Grandchildren calling our names
Early evening dinners
A glass of wine with friends
Breakfast on the deck
With sports section, crossword puzzle
Hummingbirds feeding above the wisteria

Each day
A celebration
Of arriving
Into this moment
Then always
The lift of spirit
As the adventure
Begins again

Carol

Ecstasies

Let ecstasies come very well spaced.
Let one not hide another.
So that in the enjoyment and pleasure
We are not conscious of time.

Yet let not one moment be like another.
The delicious, the wonder
Are there to be savored.
No way should a memory change the now.

Robert

From Carol's notebook: Intimacy

Robert opens doors for me, holds my chair at a restaurant table. Unlike many couples who sit in silence, we talk as we wait for salad, taste each other's entree and linger over coffee. On the street we walk hand in hand. Strangers smile as we pass as if surprised by our awareness of each other and our obvious age. I long to declare to anyone who will listen that romance is not the prerogative of the young. Falling in love in our sixties and seventies was no different for Robert and me. The feelings of romance are the same whether one is a young adult, traversing middle years or in the last decades. We are lovers. We enjoy the long slow mornings beginning with a smile. We shower together. Robert shampoos my hair. I dry his back.

Living intimately is more than touch. It is the small moments, the use of a private language, that word or phrase that evokes a tender memory. It is knowing each other's favorite color, being sensitive to moods, having an awareness of stress points, knowing tastes in food, music and books.

Sometimes when I see people react to our late love, I think back to Baden-Baden and our visit to the Roman-Irish baths. After entering, we parted to climb twin staircases. With others of our own gender we each showered, soaked, sat in rooms of dry heat and then were massaged. We met in the steam bath and stayed together in the large public pools. There was something basic and elemental about it. We were all just people. No one flaunted their nudity nor was there any sense of shame when we walked from one area to the next.

So it is with being in love in late life. Certainly there are wrinkles, age spots and thinning hair. We cherish one other as we are now, and in this realism, romance endures. We accept the gift, and live with grace.

Celebrate

Every day there is a present
Waiting for me
Wrapped in sunrise orange, Mediterranean blue
Or in tissue paper white of new snow.

Some have bows and some not.
I've seen ribbon both wide and narrow.
Some boxes are big, others are small.
Once in a while a day too big to wrap.

Who sets the scene my eyes behold
When I finally get them open?
Through your sleepy face I sense the day
And wake to all it offers.

Sharing the wonders of a new morning,
It doesn't matter how it's wrapped.
Plain paper tied with ordinary string or
In scenic splendor of castles on the Rhine.

I celebrate the moment, for we both know
"Anticipation is a judgment." I untie the knot,
Unfold the paper, lift the lid, and peek inside.
And there it is. A new unexperienced day.

Robert

Remember, My Love

The Danube on a gray morning, the Seine by Notre Dame, moonlight on the Thames, the Shire in Malawi with hippopotami and dozing crocodiles, the pension beside the river Inn that gives Innsbruck its name, ships that sail the Rhine and the Mosel, willow trees along the Cam, the Salzach, turquoise from the Alpine snow, mist rising on the Zambezi below Victoria Falls. So many shaded paths that followed water.

In Baden-Baden our square of balcony overlooks the promenade along the river Oos where Queen Victoria and Prince Albert enjoyed an evening stroll. Birds sing in shaded green. At water's edge azaleas and rhododendrons bloom, reflecting pinks and reds of setting sun. We watch the gentle patterns of the current flow past us on its journey. We talk of rivers and sip white wine.

Carol

My Beloved

My life is filled with loveliness.
You are the reason.
Being with you is full of surprises.
As soon as I think I know you,
My concept is out of date, for you change.
Then I adjust and find I am behind,
For there you go again, delighting me.

I love you and I love your achievements.
They are yours alone.
I am content to provide
A nurturing place with room
Where you are free to grow.
To share and be a part is all I ask.
If I fall behind, reach back,
Give me your hand.

Robert

We Could Never Tell Each Other

How it was to be married to someone else,
When we spoke in different languages of love,
Met another's eyes with looks of disbelief
Or in acknowledgement of some small irony.

You cannot know how I reacted to lonely midnights,
Lay awake to watch the clock slow, stop at three A.M.
Would you be surprised to learn
I could not cry when my mother died?

I can imagine you,
Brown curly hair above the perplexed frown.
Did you walk the floor, try to soothe a crying baby
Letting Libby sleep?

Where did you learn to hold me when I'm angry,
Allow me to talk as you listen,
Knowing I have no need for you to do
The knight on a white charger thing,
Try to make things right.

We have so seldom been apart.
Once you went to an office every day,
Solved problems, dictated letters.
What excited you? Formulating chemicals?
Planting roses on Saturday morning?

Sometimes I wish you could picture
How I looked as a young bride,
When I blushed easily, hid my shyness with a smile.
Or the way I walked at thirty-five
Wearing a drop-dead jumpsuit, knowing
Approving glances followed as I moved.

Our spouses died. They will never know
These years of aging.
We express our fears of disease, lingering death,
Enjoy the peace of slow Mondays,
Early dinner of the senior special,
The lovely choice of buying tickets or staying home.

When we stroll the neighborhood,
It is you who holds my hand.

Carol

From Carol's notebook: Time

When we met I was almost sixty years of age—Robert nearing seventy-one. We knew at the start of our relationship that the number of our days would count down in unstoppable cadence. We would not have a lifetime to share. Yet strangely we have known unlimited time in the ten years we have been together.

Because days do not pass unmarked, unnoticed, we can revel in the exotic atmosphere of foreign cities, the narrow cobblestone streets of Spain, the wide plazas of Florence, the blend of new and old architecture in Barcelona, all peak moments. We also delight in the quiet days in Phoenix with doves on the wall and saguaro in bloom. In the gold country of California, we sit under a summer sky of stars.

In this strange paradox of time, each day stretches long. We enjoy a full spectrum of choice on how we spend the hours. There is time to take a walk, discover a new author, play with a grandchild, write a poem. Robert works on the computer, bringing financial records up to date or exploring the Internet for recipes or travel tips. He exchanges e-mail with family and friends from around the world or across town. I hem a new pair of slacks, paint a hot air balloon on the bare bathroom wall or set a table for company with my favorite flower-strewn china. Separate but aware of the other, caught up in the slow tempo of minutes becoming hours, we plan a holiday, telephone a friend, share a chicken curry salad, listen to a Strauss waltz.

We pray to remain healthy and active, but trust that even if limitations come, we will find new opportunities to enlarge our awareness of love and the life we hold so dear. We accept the breathless pace of years whose drum-beat will not stop, and live each endless day as a song that lasts forever.

Glacier Talk

A white giant reclines against the blue
Making small talk
Little bursts of conversational air
Trapped in frozen pasts
Freed by morning sunshine
Explode to life
Shout a message....
Suddenly, in a great calving of wisdom
Giant plumes of ancient lore
Climb the arctic air

Standing with you
At the rail of the cruise ship
I want to speak glacier
I do not know the words
I long to know the secrets
Being told to sky and bay
I wish to join the dialogue
Tell how we met so late in life
Record my feelings of this world we share
Where love creates love

I will my thoughts to freeze
To sleep in secret cache
Then burst to life
In some turquoise tomorrow
Future travelers would learn
The promise of this moment
The way you smile
And how you hold my hand

Carol

Stuff

I never knew that I'd be left
To finally decide
What to do with the accumulated stuff
Of thirty-seven years and thirteen months.

Everything so precious,
I'd die if it were lost.
Boxes, full of who knows what,
A lifetime of saving
So we wouldn't forget,
Then couldn't remember where it was.

Thirty-seven years in this house.
Our kids grew up; friends moved away,
Pets, parents, and a wife who died,
Leaving me the task of letting go.

How many boxes of who knows what?
And my best memories aren't packed with all
The precious stuff.
I have learned that it's the people,
All the people I have loved
Who make me what I am.

Robert

Borobudor

Borobudor
Say it again
And again   Borobudor
Borobudor

Word becomes mantra
Canopy of jungle
Gives way to clearing
Where grey stones rise
In pyramid precision
To a circle of forever

Beyond Semerang
In unrelenting sun
It waits
I climb ancient steps
Walk each ascending level
To read the story
Carved in pictures
How Buddha lived and sought
A oneness

Borobudor
You shame me
I have left no tales in stone
Never piled them one on one
To mark a pilgrim path

I speak your name
Borobudor
And leave my story
On the Java wind

Carol

Champagne Bubbles

Champagne bubbles and dandelion fountain
Lure me back to Sydney, gateway
For a ferry ride to the race track.
A winning ticket on number nine.

From there to the Great Barrier Reef,
Sea and fish and flowers of multi hue,
To temples in Bali sheltered by the sacred mountain.
Walk where Mati Hari strolled.
Climb the steps of Borobudor.
Shop in Singapore, tour Bangkok
To marvel at the Golden Buddha
Thai palace of the king.

Champagne bubbles where will you lead?
What undiscovered fountain will be there?
Lure me back,
To walk beside a river,
In a land I do not know.

Robert

Sunday in Sydney

Sunday in Sydney
We wake to crescent rolls
Smiling on our plates
Marmalade
And tea in fat china pots

At Circular Quay
We buy tickets for the big blue bus
That tours the city
Stopping often
Allowing us to leave or board
On sudden whim

We gaze across the bay
At arch of bridge
And Opera House
Moored in sunlight
We walk in parks
Smile at people eating
Crab sandwiches
At little tables by the shore

At sunset
Our restaurant
Is a tower of glass
Above the harbor
We eat fish and lamb
Crisp potatoes
Watch lights below
Grow brighter
Then wait to guide us
Through dark
To the hotel

Days like this never end
They go on
In unbroken reach of hours
Say I can step inside
To any moment I choose
To marmalade
To you beside me on the bus
And always find you
In friendly Australian evening
Sharing forever time
Sunday in Sydney

Sunday in Sydney
With you

Carol

Pilgrimage

I step from the tour bus
Into the hot New Guinea sun,
One more silver-haired passenger
From the white ship anchored in the harbor.

I walk among five-thousand graves,
Asterisks to an almost-forgotten war.
The green of the lawn
Stretches from past sorrows
To unknown tomorrows.
I cannot walk it.
I must stand and wonder what I feel.

I look up to shrouded mountains.
This is the land my brother knew
Fifty years ago.
Was it kind to him before he fell?
Did this far island ever hear his laughter?
Did any bird sing on that last day?
What view of jungle growth filled his eyes
Before they closed forever?

I think of Jim as he was
Striding up the walk from college
Tennis racket in hand,
Smiling when he won his match.
I still see him
In the evening
Swaying with the music of his violin.

In this instant his image is more real
Than the grass or the mountains
Or the shaded headstone beneath my hand,
The one marked
"Unknown Airman, 1945."

Carol

From Robert's notebook: African Impressions

The most fascinating aspect of our travels has been the opportunity to observe, be with, and when possible to talk to the people we have encountered. To describe Africa in a few words—we found it remarkable that the people could live in poverty with so much pride. The dirt or gravel surrounding the rondevals or huts is swept so clean that it appears more like a movie set rather than a place where natives live. The people walk straight and erect for miles to go to market or return to the village of their birth when the chief or other notable dies. Merchants enjoy bargaining for their wares to the point that they are willing to trade a carving that took many days for a tee shirt or a week's work for a pair of white shoes in order to look nice.

The exotic experiences in Bothuthatswana, Malawi, South Africa, and Zimbabwe challenged all the five senses. How could I describe the sensations to someone who had never been here?

Open your eyes to behold an orange sunrise sky reflected in the surface of Lake Kariba. The sight of a hundred natives waiting in line to fill every imaginable container with paraffin (kerosene) from a tank truck. Watch a beautiful woman dressed in orange and black African print as she raises her arm with open palm in friendly salute.

Savor the taste of a breakfast of biscuit sandwiches with ham and scrambled eggs accompanied by gin and tonic on a boat that resembles "African Queen" in the middle of the River Shire in Malawi chugging past crocodiles, hippopotami and deep-blue water hyacinths. In South Africa eat crayfish as big and as delightful as a three-pound Maine lobster while overlooking the Indian Ocean. The following afternoon delight in a picnic lunch of crisp apples, smooth pate, cold Chardonnay on the lawn of an estate winery.

Hold your ears to shut out some of the roar of the water coming over Victoria Falls. Then strain to hear the swish of elephants pulling grass as they feed at night. Smile at the "Last night in Kansas City" call of the doves compared to our mournful cooing birds. Experience the excitement of a lion's roar even when you know it's miles away.

Driving through the sugar cane fields, smell the dirt roadways that are sprayed with molasses to control the dust. The pungent odor of bright tropical fish when spread on nets to dry in the sun. The aroma of barbecued chicken awaiting as you walk towards a large tree-house following a canoe trip down river on a game farm. The fragrance of a newly opened plumeria blossom.

Reach through the chain-link fence to feel the unbelievable strength underlying the coat of a three-year-old lioness. Revel in the refreshment of a shower with rock walls open to a star-filled sky. Feel the smooth wood of a carved elephant or a dancing family in stone. Finally the warmth in the handshake of the airport guard before boarding the plane for home.

African Night

Just before sleep
In a lodge
On the edge of Lake Kariba
In Zimbabwe
In the dark of African night

I feel
More than hear
Hear without seeing
The elephants
The elephants approach.

First, a whisper
Like leaves in wind
The last sigh before dreams
Swish of scythe cutting hay

The elephants come
Feeding as they walk
Grass torn from soil
Uprooted in clumps
Huge trunks sway
Seeking shoots of green

Outside the lodge
Outside in blackness
A dead branch snaps
Then another
Loud and louder
Each crack an explosion

I feel
More than hear
Hear without seeing
The grey shape of fear
As elephants pass
On the edge of Lake Kariba
In Zimbabwe
In the dark
Of African night

Carol

The High Clear Room of Zimbabwe

It's sixty miles
to Mozambique
with no walls to block
the view. At night
there's the Milky Way
for a ceiling
and the Big Dipper
is upside down.
The Man in the Moon
is a rabbit.

The Southern Cross
could guide us—
but the lodge is
just steps away.

Robert

Sukuru

In Zimbabwe, near the city of Harare,
We walked among stone sculptures
In the garden of the artist.
Our guide, a young black man,
Addressed Robert as "Sukuru,"
A title honoring his seventy-five years.

We paused to study each rendering—
Man and woman beneath their totem of a bear,
Eagle poised for flight,
Dung beetle, intent upon his task,
The face of a young girl—

"You wish to buy, Sukuru?
I make you special price."

We chose a small figure of green stone
Which Robert carried to the car.
The guide asked about our home.
I talked of California,
Of red bougainvillaea by the door,
Purple flowering jacaranda.

"You are fortunate to have a man
Who is Sukuru.
No one in Africa, my age,
Can hope to live so long."

The unsaid word,
That named disease
Hung in the air between us.
I, an aging woman from America,
What could I say to change his truth?

I turned, walked back to the gate.
He followed, waved his hand,
"Goodbye, Madam. Goodbye, Sukuru."

Half a world away,
I hold the small male figure,
Carved in stone.
I weep for the young man.

It is his face I see.

Carol

From Carol's notebook: Gifts

I have walked among open stalls in distant flea markets. Wandered through specialty stores in Sydney and Singapore, admired cashmere sweaters, fringed shawls, imagined the gleam of a silver bracelet on the wrist of a granddaughter.

Age has lessened my own need for possessions. Most clothing is designed for long-legged, slender young women. With my almost-white hair I shun earth colors, golds, bronzes, even cool pastels. I scan racks of apparel, only once in a while finding some garment that will click into place in my wardrobe, something new that I can wear like an old and favorite garment.

Mostly I shop for presents. I shop for birthdays and Christmas no matter how far in the future. I look for that sudden find I hope will delight someone I cherish. I love to watch the stash of gifts grow. I enjoy the wrapping and the presentation.

I feel sorry for people who find no joy in Christmas, see it as a series of tasks to endure. I love all celebrations. The child in me always delights in moments of pink balloons and glowing candles.

In April of 1998 Robert enjoyed his eightieth birthday. His daughter Nansie and her husband Ray came from Africa to be with him. His son Richard flew from Minneapolis to join Blair, the youngest son, his wife Marjorie and daughter Ashley who live near us in Phoenix. For almost a year, they had planned this surprise. Four wonderful days of marvelous meals, sushi and teppan in a Japanese restaurant, our favorite fajita platters at the local Mexican restaurant. The food extravaganza was highlighted by a birthday dinner at Blair and Margie's home with specially prepared asparagus, steak with Roquefort, mushrooms and ice cream cake, wicked with crunches of coffee beans and chocolate. There were presents to open, but the best gift of all was the gift of Robert's family—the taking time to be with him, the smiles, the conversations, the expressions of love.

Remembering those days as I shop for presents, I realize that nothing material replaces the giving of one's self. I hope that the presents I choose reflect the joy I felt in their selection and remain tangible evidence of my love. I pray to be responsive when someone needs a hug, a quiet conversation, a night out while I play with grandchildren or my presence at a graduation.

On a wall at home in Phoenix, a framed motto reads "What we are is God's gift to us. What we become is our gift to God."

Hey, I Am Eighty

What's it like to be eighty?
Is it supposed to be different?
The sun comes up nice and bright
In about a week the moon will be full.

I just celebrated a birthday full of love,
With my kids from Zimbabwe, Minneapolis
And just up the hill.
Kids you ask, when only the youngest
Can look forward to being fifty.

One daughter, two sons keeping secrets
Since last October and some say July.
Flying all the way to be the surprise
That took my breath away.

So what's it like to be eighty?
Great when you are loved
And able to love right back.

Robert

Conversation

In our room
At the Imperial Hotel in Kyoto
We wrapped ourselves in blue kimonos
Patterned with wide-winged birds
Sat on floor cushions
Instead of proper chairs
Sipped green tea
From little china cups without handles

On the bathroom wall
The roll of toilet paper
Ended in perfect point of white
I took the fan-shaped soap
From the red box printed gold

A phone hung on the wall above the tub
As I soaked in jasmine-scented water
I phoned my sister in California
Her idea of travel is a stroll
Down a hill of lawn in her backyard
To a lounge chair
Shaded by young redwood trees
There she spends hours
With books on philosophy

I described treasures already packed
Carved candlesticks, Kabuki dolls
Batik prints and lengths of real Thai silk
Asked what she would like
As souvenir. She could not decide

So we talked of temple bells
Monks in yellow robes
And how before a prayer is said
One bows, claps hands
To call the Gods

Carol

Treasure in Saint Thomas

Beside the bay
Charlotte Amalie
Stirs, wakens
Tourists parade like shore birds
Plump and brightly plumed

Each jewelry store
Promises the lowest price
Highest quality
Every door stands open
Smiling clerks wave hands
Above trays of smug emeralds
Modest aquamarines
I will not be deterred by
Gleam of sapphires, blaze of opals
Or pause to admire an elite tanzanite ring
Blue-violet dream, guarded by diamonds

We walk past the counters luring me to gold
I know bracelets, necklaces by name
Sedusa, Byzantine, San Marcos and Omega.
I recognize the soft patina of ten-
And fourteen-carat designs
Brazen yellow of Italian gold
Boasting its higher count

I do not stop
It is the pearls that beckon
Real pearls, survivors of living dark
I do not wish the baroque
Nor expensive gray or hint of pink
There, the creamy strand, thirty-two inches in length
I roll it across the white satin pad
Each globe, smooth, warm under my touch
The salesman invites me to bite the necklace
Prove its origin
With the feel of grit from sea between my teeth

I hold the pearls to my neck
See face reflected above
Can I wear my days in such a way
String them one by one
Make each irritation another
Shining moment
We buy the pearls
Inside my purse
They rest in velvet bag
Another treasure
Like sunshine in Saint Thomas
And Robert's smile

Carol

Pack Up All Our Love

The ad reads:
Love is all you need
Everything's included for couples at one single price
Relax on the Caribbean's finest white sand beaches
Luxuriate in ultra suites
Experience every land and water sport
Savor anytime snacks
Unlimited premium-brand drinks
38 gourmet restaurants
And be moved by a staff as warm as the Caribbean sun
All inclusive
All in the name of love.

Do you suppose, my Dear,
It is like the ad?
Can you pack enough of our zest for life
And far-off places in two suitcases?

We will need traveler's checks.
It is a "Two for One," so only bring a few.
Put in swimsuits even though we probably
Won't relax on their white sand beach.
By the way, how do we "luxuriate in ultra suites?"
Bet it can't be better than the Regent or the
Other 355 beds we've shared.

Hope you have room for fishing tackle
Clubs and bowling ball because
I would hate to miss a sport.
Wonder if we can have our anytime snacks
On a balcony like that afternoon
Overlooking the Oos in Baden-Baden?
Unlimited premium-brand drinks, nothing
Tastes better than Chandon on a cruise.

There are 38 gourmet restaurants in a week.
Remember paella on the hilltop in Altea, Spain,
Haggis at Blairinnie Farm in Crossmichael, Scotland?
The staff is going to be warm by the time
They move us around before our stay is over.

All in the name of love? All inclusive?
I don't think there is any connection
Between what we feel and this Madison Avenue concept.
Besides all the luggage in the world wouldn't
Begin to hold all the love I have for you.
Come put your arms around me, give me a kiss.

Oh, call the 800 number,
See if they have a senior discount.

Robert

Me an Ocean?

If I could be the oceans and all the seas
I would be vast enough to give you love
So deep, you could not doubt I care.

If you were a ship riding high above my depths
I would provide strong currents and prevailing winds
To guide you to a gentle bay, a safe harbor.

Where breezes are warmed by tropic sun,
Tranquil waves break on sandy beach,
Sunsets are a wonder to behold.

You would never see my stormy side
Never have to endure rain and wind
If I could be the oceans and all the seas.

Robert

From Carol's notebook: Santa Barbara Writers Conference

The last full week of June, in our room overlooking the Pacific Ocean

We have arrived early, made this space our own, computer set on desk, a rented-for-the-week small refrigerator stocked with breakfast and lunch essentials, table by the window where we will talk and write, share our creative bursts.

This afternoon bubbles large and small drift across our view. They sparkle in the afternoon sun, pop and disappear into the soft sea air. I walk on the terrace, look down the boardwalk, see a young woman entertaining a small boy and girl. I do not need the explanation—the unusual always happens at the writers conference.

This week we live in a world of words, spoken, written, crossed out, replaced. We will attend lectures, workshops, read our early drafts for criticism, listen to another's work in progress. Each year, returning writers grow dearer. We have known their sorrows and laughter as they dared to share their life in lines on paper.

As we struggle with words of our own, some shining idea will drift into our awareness, enlarging perceptions. For now we have each other, this familiar room, the view of sand and sea and our expectations, as fragile as bubbles.

The Wolf Who Cried "Boy"

How come I get all the bad press?
Granted, there has to be a villain,
Maybe a white hat is not my style,
But just for once, can't I be me?

I appear at casting, dressed in fancy duds.
Today they're handing out
Sheep skins still covered with wool
With ears, nose and toothless grins.

Reminds me of a year ago or was it two?
When I spent a month developing my lungs,
So my huff and puff would blow in houses.
What a mess! What would you expect in a pig's abode?

When the huffin' and puffin' failed
They wanted me to climb down the chimney.
I was surprised I wasn't asked to dress
Like Santa Claus with red suit and bowl of jelly.

That wasn't the end of it
Next, I had to put on Granny's nightie
Wait for a babe all dressed in red
Showed up praising my ears, nose and teeth.

I wonder what might have happened
As I was sure she was about to climb in bed
When this macho hunter with a blunderbuss
Made me drop the basket and run like hell.

They made me give back Granny's gear.
What a shame 'cause who could ever know,
I might have found a starring role
Dancing with a dude named Kevin Costner.

Still, somehow it all seems so unfair
That casting for Aesop and Mother Goose
Put us wolves in such poor light.
Just once, I'd like to be the one to kiss the girl.

Robert
(Award winner at Santa Barbara Writers Conference)

Cashmere Sweaters and Other Friends

Cream-colored shirts hum to me.
Purple raincoats know my name.
I swim in the blues and greens of scarves,
Surrender to seduction of perfume and scented creams.
I love being near four-hundred-dollar dresses
With peach chiffon personalities.
Black pumps dressed up with satin bows
Tell me where to go for dinner,
And I never met any blue lingerie
I did not like.

Sometimes I hug a fake fur coat,
Pose in red hat with ribbons hanging down,
Smile at blue jeans,
Lean close to smell a new leather bag.

Then I buy shorts for Bob,
A toy tractor for Ryan,
Go home,
Put on my pink robe
That has loved me
Ever since we met
One January sale.

> *Carol*
> *(Award winner at Santa Barbara Writers Conference)*

The Love I Feel

In writing of the power of love,
I failed to modify or define.
Didn't use the adjective unconditional.

If I still have not made myself clear,
consider it in the sense of unqualified,
with the synonyms unrestricted, unlimited,
unmitigated, unreserved, and without reserve.

Is there a tendency to doubt?
How about implicit, unquestioning, undoubting,
unhesitating or would I be better understood
with explicit, express, clear, unmistakable?

Wait, there are more words to consider,
peremptory, categorical, unequivocal,
indisputable, and unappealable. And as the
Bible states "Love is the fulfilling of the law."

Love that I have been given for eighty years
Has been positive, absolute, definite, definitive,
determinate, decided, decisive, fixed, and final.
But not final in the sense of being at an end.

Then the surprise of Roget when unconditional
calls forth the two words: round and flat.
Webster rescues with round as complete or full.
Flat as clear and unmistakable.

Or in the vernacular—complete, entire, total, utter,
perfect, downright, outright, out-and-out, straight,
straight-out, all-out, and to listen to my grandkids
flat-out has found its way into our language.

I may not always choose the best words,
to describe the love I feel and want to give,
with my mind, my heart, and soul,
A perfect love full of surprises.

Robert

Remembering Ice

I like happy-ever endings. I believe the old cliches, the rainbows after rain-drops, clouds with silver linings, and I know that Rhett went back again to Scarlet and flowers bloomed at Tara once again.

I like a present tied with ribbon, know it waits upon a table for my touch. I never rush the opening. I untie the bow so slowly, and if there is a knot, my fingers play with it, until it loosens and falls free. I peel back each piece of tape and leave the paper whole, with the crisp folds remembering where the box was held. And the gift inside is perfect, for I know that it was chosen just for me.

I like window seats in airplanes. You will see me there, my nose against the glass, thinking of pioneers, the mountains and the rivers that they crossed. Now I fly above them all as if I were a god. I know the joy of looking down on clouds.

If asked about my life, I could talk of the three "D's", divorce, disease and death. But it's all a kind of journey, I bought tickets with my tears. I never found the price to be too high. I could quote aloud from scripture, Psalm number twenty-three. Remember just one word, the word is "through." Through the valley of the shadow where happy endings wait and the celebra-tion starts when you know the trip is over, and you are Dorothy back in Kan-sas on the farm.

Why am I the lucky person who finds the parking space, who wins the prize that's raffled at the fair, who always seems to be a step beyond the hurt?

That night in Santa Barbara, we shared smorgasbord at Scandia near the mountain where the fire began. Lights above our table flickered then went out. We skipped dessert and drove to the hotel, away from all the yellow smoke, the sirens' piercing cries. The ice machine was out of order. We went to find another, between the cottages, past the empty tennis courts. The breeze blowing from the ocean felt fresh and cool.

While in the hills, with hot white fury, the fire raged on and on. We walked back to our room—carrying the ice.

Carol

First Cast

White mist hides
Surface of the lake.
Pine trees take shape,
Sentinels of dawn.

Silence is broken by the
Swish of line running through
Guides of steel and gentle splash
As float and bait hit water.

Rod rests gently in the notch
Of a newly cut willow branch.
The line hangs limp and just in sight,
Time to rub hands for warmth.

Imperceptibly the line moves
Slowly begins to tighten.
Tip of pole yields to pressure.
I take the rod from its cradle.

Wait a second for
Right moment to pull back.
Set the hook. Shout "Fish On"
Though no one hears.

I have a good one,
Play him carefully.
No horsing this one in. The splash,
As he breaks water, confirms his size.

Who can know how long it took to
Bring this trout to shore.
At last he lies at my feet,
In shallow ripples of the lake.

Slipping my fingers behind his gills,
I lift the fish from the water.
Eighteen inches of silver beauty,
A rainbow for my creel.

Robert

Thank You Note

At first, you wrote letters
Then came to me, poems in hand.
We told our stories to one another,
Pondered menus at corner tables,
Lingered after dinner
Sharing dreams.

Sometimes, we sing old romantic songs,
Remember almost-forgotten lyrics.
I delight to hear you speak my name,
Chuckle at my puns,
Tell me your opinions,
Solemnly consider the correct letters
For the daily crossword puzzle.

You punctuate my evening
When you look up from your book,
Read aloud the flight of words
That lifts your spirit.

Your "good mornings" and "good nights"
Are the bookends of each day.

Thank you, my dear,
For entering my silence,
For bringing back the words.

Carol

Choice

On the one hand I like the silence
To be with you and not have to relate

On the other hand I want to talk
Hear what you have to say

On the one hand I would rather stay home
Do some things that long to be done

On the other hand let's get up and go
Be part of the wonderful.

Robert

From Robert's notebook: Aging

In August of 1988 I found a quotation in an Ann Landers column from "Life Begins at 80" by Frank Laubach which reads in part "I have good news for you. The first 80 years are the hardest. The second 80 are a succession of birthday parties."

1998 was the year of my eightieth birthday and the whole twelve months were one big celebration with numerous parties. As soon as someone learned that I had reached that milestone they were anxious to congratulate me, buy me a drink, pick up a check, or find some way to add to my pleasure by expressing theirs. Reflecting back on this year I feel that describing life at eighty as "a succession of birthday parties" is inadequate and comes up short of symbolizing all of the happenings in the fifteen years since my retirement.

In July while on a European trip we were invited for dinner with Carol's cousin by marriage in Horsens, Denmark. It was an evening that we will always remember as the wine and food and fellowship were without limit. As Inga served each dish or refilled our glasses of wine, she said "Don't forget there is always more in the kitchen." Later that night I woke up and realized that phrase expresses the way it has become for me. Life is so good, so full of love, happiness, pleasure, and satisfaction that I really don't have to ask for more. But it is reassuring to know that should I have a need, "There's more in the kitchen."

Then I begin to wonder why is it my good fortune to have a companion, friends, relatives, and casual acquaintances with such full kitchens who are so willing to share with me. I am thankful for good health and the lack of pressure that permits us the luxury of travel and time to explore kitchen cupboards all around the world as well as our own home. I wish everyone could be as fortunate.

Path

Where does this path lead?
To pathfinder? No, that's who I am.
Pathos, that's not where I want to go.
This way to pathology. Not for me.
I'll just walk on and see.
Pathetic, you must be kidding.
But wait. The synonym trail reads
Affecting, moving, emotional, tender, melting—
And that sounds just right for me.

Robert

Privilege of Tears

I have been young and I have been ancient.
I know the sweet kiss of the summertime rain,
The hope that is morning, the deep peace of midnight
The sudden sharp sting, the announcement of pain.

All that is human I hold as a lover.
Each sorrow is teacher. I learn from my fears.
I will give thanks for exuberant moments,
For the grace to be joyful, the privilege of tears.

Carol

Ode to my Atrial Flutter

The nurse says it's time for your EKG
And puts on the cold electrodes.
Oh, you atrial flutter with variable AV block,
How you louse up a rhythmical beat.

Why can't you disappear like you did
The four times your home was stopped?
It was such a relief to have you gone
And have a sinus rhythm to my beat.

But back you steal like a prodigal son.
No longer is my pulse aboom-aboom-aboom.
It's now aboom-aboom—pause—aboom,
Followed by a mooba and another pause.

I wish my chart would read normal EKG
Instead of ST abnormality with possible digitalis effect.
Oh you atrial flutter with variable AV block,
Please let me be. You go your way, I'll go mine.

Robert

Journey Between Pansies

I wish I could slip inside
This pansy
Wallow in its yellow secrets.
I would be more yellow than sunlight
Smell more yellow than lemons
The wind would teach me yellow music
Sung in long meadows of mustard

I travel on in my pansy
Circle down and around into green
To the green hollow green of the stem
Where the push of the green
And the pulse of the green
Makes the green create green
Above ground

Then I wind and weave into whiteness
Descend to the heart of a root
Follow its tapering course
Emerge from one feather-like finger
To rest
Suspended
In clouds of black loam

I crawl into another white tendril
Climb the cool pallid wall of the root
Seek the warmth as I climb to the green
Arrive on a pansy so purple
I become more purple than the most purple plum
Settle on one velvet-like petal
Tuck the twilight about me
Surrender to purple
To bliss

Carol

Freedom

I who have never been confined or
Held against my will or hardly
Ever had a wish denied,
Am delighted with newfound freedom.

To be so free that I can ask for anything
Not be concerned if the time or place is right
To truly believe that what I say or
The way I act will always be understood

Robert

Candles

In the Cathedral of Notre Dame, I light a candle for my daughter, Lee. Robert and I have traveled for three weeks, and I don't know how she is. She lives beyond sadness, in seasons of depression. I always know exactly how she feels by the way she says "Hello" when answering the phone. Now, so far away, I can only watch the flame and pray for her a birthday party face, the kind she wore when she was seven, the year she cut her pony tail, received a two-wheeled bike. I think of her two brothers, years of chocolate cakes with candles. The five of us, a family, as we lit each special taper on so many advent wreaths.

Candles always make me think of Clare, and the Christmas parties, years of Christmas parties in her house that overlooked Los Gatos and the California Hills. One December, we counted ninety-nine red candles—on the tables set for dinner, in the high arched windows of the hall, in the green of holly on the mantelpiece and the dark reflective surface of the baby grand. Clare moved to a condominium. Gene, Mark, Harold, Erik, Earl, Dick, John and Fred, who once sang their joy in carols—all have died.

I like the cliché of candlelight on little corner tables, the shared bottle of Domain Chandon Cuvee, small bouquets of roses, the orchestra that plays "our song"—all supposed to be romantic and for me, it is always true. I am even sentimental over earthquakes, like that bad one in October; it rumbled through a little before dark. Without electric power, we filled the room with candles, cut some bread and cheese and opened up the wine. We talked and talked for hours and never knew the lights came on in about twenty minutes' time.

If I pass you in my car, note the license plate, it reads "IN LIGHT." So, you see. I have my ways of holding back the dark.

Carol

Life Style

England in April
In our rental car
We leave the crowded M road
Clogged with lines of lorries
Impatient drivers

We wander through green hills
Partridges fly from hedge rows
Daffodils watch as we pass

We stop for a proper tea
Scones and jam and clotted cream
Talk to shopkeepers, buy a gift
Walk the narrow cobbled street

We cannot find this village on our map
Or know which obscure sign
Will point our way
It does not matter
We are together

The mist lifts
Every road leads to daffodils

Carol

As the British Do

In a car, passengers sit between
A bonnet and a boot.
When on holiday one stops
At eleven for brandy and coffee
And again at four for tea.

We wanted to be considerate of
Differences and not offend.
But the sign "Avoid the scree and
Stay out of the beck in spate"
Really didn't make much sense.

English friends were quick to explain.
The scree is loose rock, beck the stream
In spate means in flood and little lambs eat ivy.
But the pub is open. It's time for fun.
That's the same everywhere.

Robert

From the Hotel in Sandown

This new spring day
Mist hugs the curve of beach
Cows pose on horizon
Of green hills
From a roadside stand
We buy pink and blue
Anemones
Find Irish linen in
A little shop beside the quay

In the restaurant
Above the market
You eat a dozen raw oysters
From a blue pottery plate
I savor white wine
Salmon wrapped in filo
Strangers pause at our table
Wish us good journey home

Next week in
California
We will revel in the
Dear, the familiar
Find celebration and excitement
In ordinary days
As we remember
How at home we are

Today
In the peace of Sandown
On the Isle of Wight

Carol

Passing Places

From Ullapool
Beyond Inverness
We choose the seldom
Traveled road
Pass hidden lochs
Through glen of fern
Where stone ruins of crofters' cabins
Sleep like forgotten dreams

In purple heather
We climb the long slope of mountain
The road narrows to one lane
With no room to overtake
Or journey by another car
Unless a turn is made
Into a passing place
A half circle where one
Waits for the other
Then continues on alone

At the moment of meeting
Always a smile, a wave
A celebration
That for this time the
Road is not so empty
Then, the passing completed
Each goes his separate way
To disappear in Scottish mist

You and I
traveled far to share
This time
This passing place
This moment in our lives
To meet
With fern and loch
And heather-shrouded hills
To know the joy of one another
Before the parting
Before the dark enfolds

Carol

About Roses

We live in a house of reflected roses
In chintz of twin couches
Captured in the gilt-framed mirror
In wallpaper of the guest room
Where granddaughters whisper wild dreams
And immediate hopes

On the sideboard
Roses are etched on crystal plate
That holds Venetian glass candies
Bought one morning in Messina

In the bedroom
Behind the bronze sculpture of a young girl
Pink slats of window blind
Match the faded petals
In bowl of potpourri
Whose perfume drifts through rooms
Urged on by gently whirring fans
Poised in high, white ceilings

You return from your errands
Even after so brief an absence
I delight in seeing you.
I am filled with the scent
Softness
Perfection of love
I accept the bouquet of roses
From your outstretched hand

Carol

We Pause to Reflect

Epilogue—1999

"I will love you yesterday as much as I have loved you tomorrow."

—Carol

"I await with eagerness what happens next."

—Robert

My Dearest Robert,

Over dinner at the Marriott in Palm Desert, we decided how to end our book. Because our relationship began with writing one another, as an epilogue we will each compose a letter to the other expressing our feelings nearly eleven years into our journey.

Remember with me how visiting Lake Louise was part of an early dream, yet we never described the actual event in written words.

We had spent two weeks in Canada, enjoying the fall colors. Driving down from Jasper towards Banff we spontaneously stopped at the Chalet, asked about a reservation and splurged on a lakeside room. In the early evening we sampled crisp chardonnay and fruity cabernet in the little wine bar. Later an orchestra played our favorite big band music while we ate dinner. We danced between courses.

At three in the morning we woke to magic, the first winter storm of the season with snowflakes frolicking in the light from the chalet. After breakfast in the sunshine of a new day, we found the ice cream sign, beds of orange-red geraniums, trimmed greenery in the hotel gardens, fir trees around the lake and mountains beyond, all covered in pristine white. We had time to walk, climb a wooded path, feel the snow chunk against our shoulders, dampen our cheeks as we played in this sudden winter fairyland.

I write of this now because it is so indicative of all our times together. Our dreams become reality as each experience takes on a dream-like quality. We have been able to let life happen, never tried to twist our days into a preset form; as a result every happening becomes greater than imagined. I am freer being with you than I could have been alone. Every moment we share is fun, exquisite, fragile, cherished. We do not try to hold them. Each becomes part of the next and the next.

I feel blessed beyond belief as our yesterdays and tomorrows blend into this eternal time, this shining present.

I have loved you, Robert, and I will love you—now and now and now.

Carol

July 1, 1999

My Darling,
At today's end we will have spent 3,888 days together which is taking into account the thirty-six days we were apart that first year. In my letter, almost eleven years ago, I wrote that I wanted to come into your life and live in the world you and I would build. I felt then and feel now that each of us brought unbelievable riches from our years of growing, and we have added the fascination of new love into developing the wonder of a new relationship.

I owe much to you. You are always open, so aware and adaptable to change. You often say that you react to your emotion or "gut feeling." You are so right that sometimes I feel I cannot keep up with your woman's intuition. I often find myself playing the "devil's advocate" with some of your decisions, and I hope that role does not bother you. It is my way of making sure that we talk things out. I always want to be a sounding board. Know I will always be there with my support.

In your letter you describe the new snow at Lake Louise. What about our two days in Paris, that sunset at the Grand Canyon, root beer floats in Wikieup, Arizona, sunrise at Lake Malawi, waterfalls in Austria, and looking down on our cruise ship from high above a Norwegian fjord? Just a few of thousands of outstanding moments that we have experienced. I will never forget your saying when we are lost, the next corner might put us on track again, and if not we will share a new experience or find a stand selling "Eis mit Schlag." So it has been for all these years.

I wish I had words at my command to tell you how much I love you. How grateful I am for the care and love you have given me. I came to San Jose hoping to find someone exactly like you. Why am I so lucky? I concluded my letter of October 31, 1988: "With those thoughts, fantasies, and a lot of promises I come to you with open heart, mind, and soul, each running on empty, but eagerly anticipating being filled to overflowing." I do not run on empty now but I am not full. With open heart, mind, and soul I await with eagerness what happens next.

I love you,
Robert